second edition

I0571056

Explore Music

a beginning activity book for kids

Kay Lowry

Cover illustration by Andrea West

ISBN 979-8-9901486-0-4

Front cover image by Andrea West
Book design by Kay Lowry

Printed and bound in the United States of America.
First printing 2023.

visit www.pianomusicforkids.com

Stillwater, Oklahoma

Table of Contents

Chapter One:

EXPLORE RHYTHM!

This is a whole note.
A whole note gets 4 beats!

Can you draw a whole note in the box?

This is a half note.

A half note gets two beats!

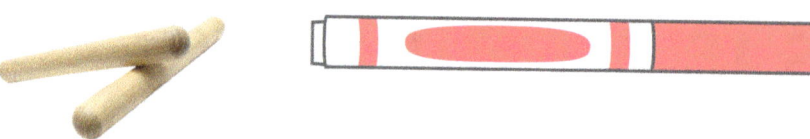 

Can you draw two half notes?

Place one in each section of the box.

This is a quarter note:

A quarter note gets one beat!

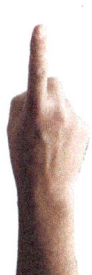

Draw four quarter notes!
Place one in each box.

This is a whole rest.

It looks like someone dug a HOLE in the ground!
A whole rest gets four beats of silence!

Can you draw a whole rest?

This is a half rest.

It looks like a hat!
A half rest gets two beats of silence!

Can you draw two half rests?

Place one in each section of the box.

This is a quarter rest.
A quarter rest gets one beat of silence!

Trace the quarter rest.

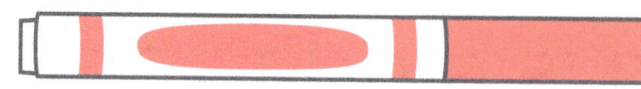

Draw four quarter rests.

Place one in each box.

Click on the QR code to check out the video and play along!

Grab some sticks or spoons to play along. Can you make a shaker?

Draw your own rhythms!
Make four beats in each box!

Go outside!

Grab some sidewalk chalk and
draw some rhythms on your driveway or sidewalk!

Chapter Two:

EXPLORE PIANO KEYS!

Use the QR code to hear a story about twin girls!

Can you circle all of the groups of 2 black keys?

Next, draw a C, D, and E on the keyboard above.

Check your work!

Use the QR code to hear a story about triplet boys!

Can you circle all of the groups of 3 black keys?

Next, draw a F, G, A, and B on the keyboard above.

Check your work!

Here are the names of all the keys!

Can you color the
keys using the code below?

C = **GREEN**

D = **YELLOW**

E = **RED**

F = **PINK**

G = **ORANGE**

A = **BLUE**

B = **PURPLE**

READY TO PLAY A GAME?

Use the QR code to
watch the video and learn how to play!

Your turn!

You will need:;

 dice

 7 small pencil top erasers, or

 small objects like lego blocks

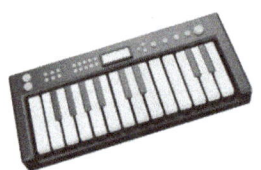 a piano or a keyboard

And this code:
1=A or G, 2=B, 3=C, 4=D, 5=E, 6=F,

Keep rolling and placing erasers on piano keys
until you have covered all seven letters!

On the piano,
when we use all the music
alphabet letters,
we start over again with "A".

We can spell words
with the music alphabet letters!
Here's one:

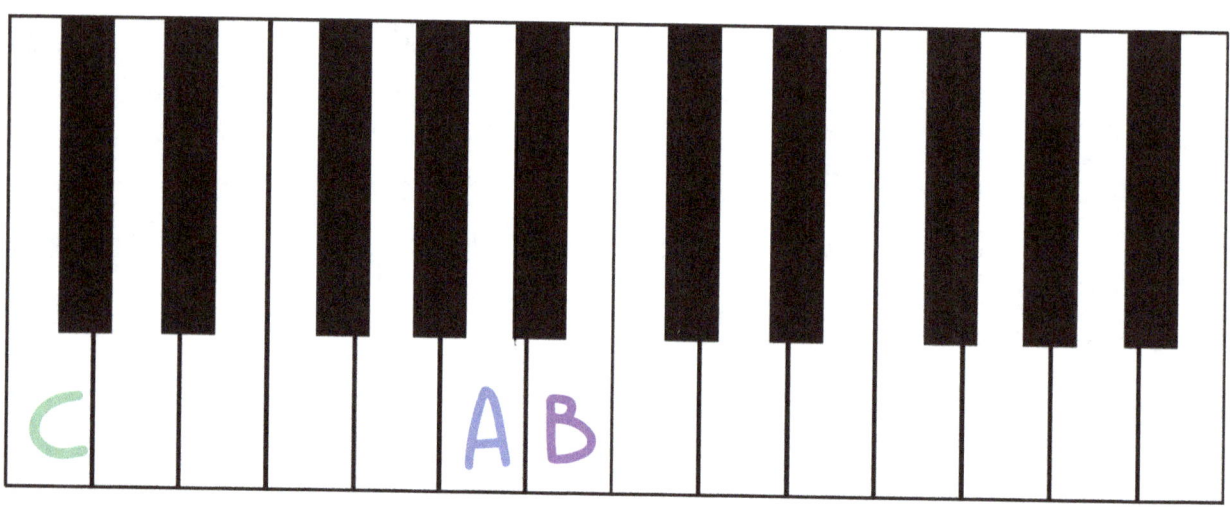

Play these keys, from left to right.
Do you like the sound?

Use your pencil
or marker to make your own
music alphabet word!
Remember,
only use letters A-G!

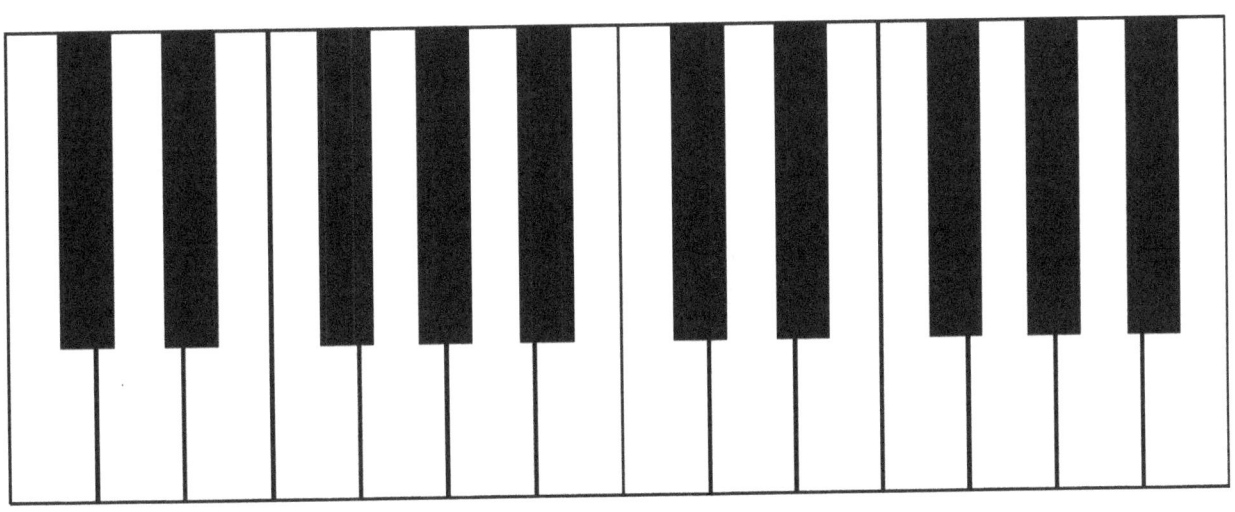

Draw your musical alphabet word on the keys, from
left to right. Play the sounds!

Chapter Three:

EXPLORE LINES, SPACES AND THE STAFF!

A musical staff has 5 lines!

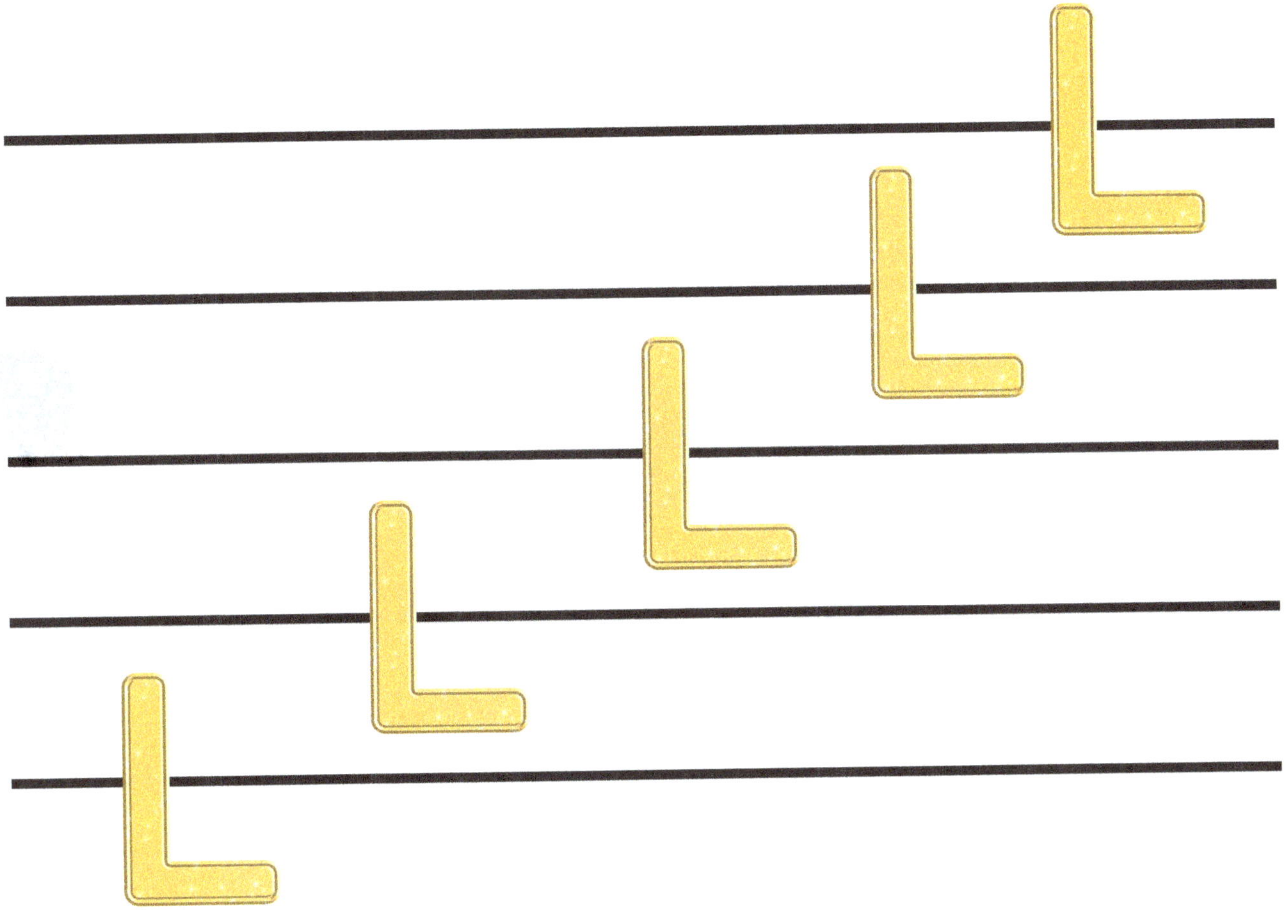

The letter "L"s are on the lines. Each line cuts through the middle of the letter.

The "circle" part of a note is called the notehead.

See how the lines cut through the middle of these whole notes? These notes are each ON a line.

When YOU draw a whole note, you will simply make a circle!

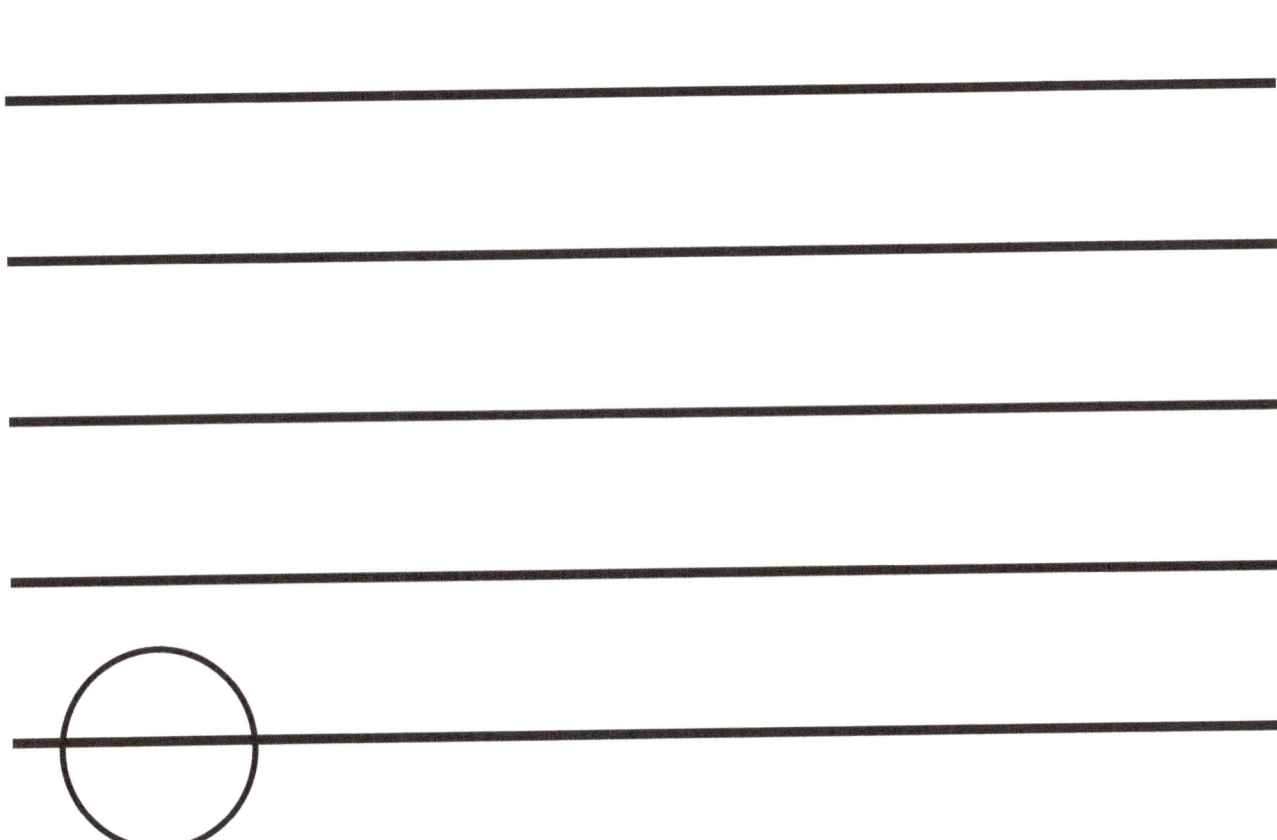

Can you trace around the first whole note, and draw a whole note on each line?

A musical staff has 4 spaces!

The letter "S"s are in between the lines. That is called a "space".

These whole notes are in between the lines. They are each ON a space.

When YOU draw a whole note, you will simply make a circle!

Can you trace around the first whole note, and draw a whole note on each space? Stay between the lines!

Game time!

You will need:

 dice

 9 small pencil top erasers, or

 small objects like buttons, or coins

And the staff on the next page!

(be sure your objects can fit
between the lines of the staff)

Here is your game board.

First, roll your dice. Look at the dots.

If you roll a 1, 3, or 5 - put one of your objects on a line.

If you roll a 2, 4, or 6 - put your object on a space.

Can you put an object on every line and space of the staff?

Chapter Four:

EXPLORE THE TREBLE CLEF!

This is a staff with a treble clef.

A treble clef is also called a "G" clef. The biggest part of the clef curls around the "G" line. On this page, the "G" line is marked in green.

Trace your finger on the G line.

When we see a clef, we know that each line or space now has a letter name.

The letter names of the treble clef spaces spell a word - FACE.

Can you write the letter names of the treble clef spaces?

44

Now can you draw a whole note (circle) on an "F" and a "C"?

Can you draw a whole note (circle) on an "A" and a "E"?

We can find the names of the lines by counting forwards and backwards in the musical alphabet.

When we go **down** on the staff, we count **backwards** to find the note name.

When we go **up** on the staff, we count **forwards** to find the note name.

Your turn! Can you write the letter name inside the whole note?

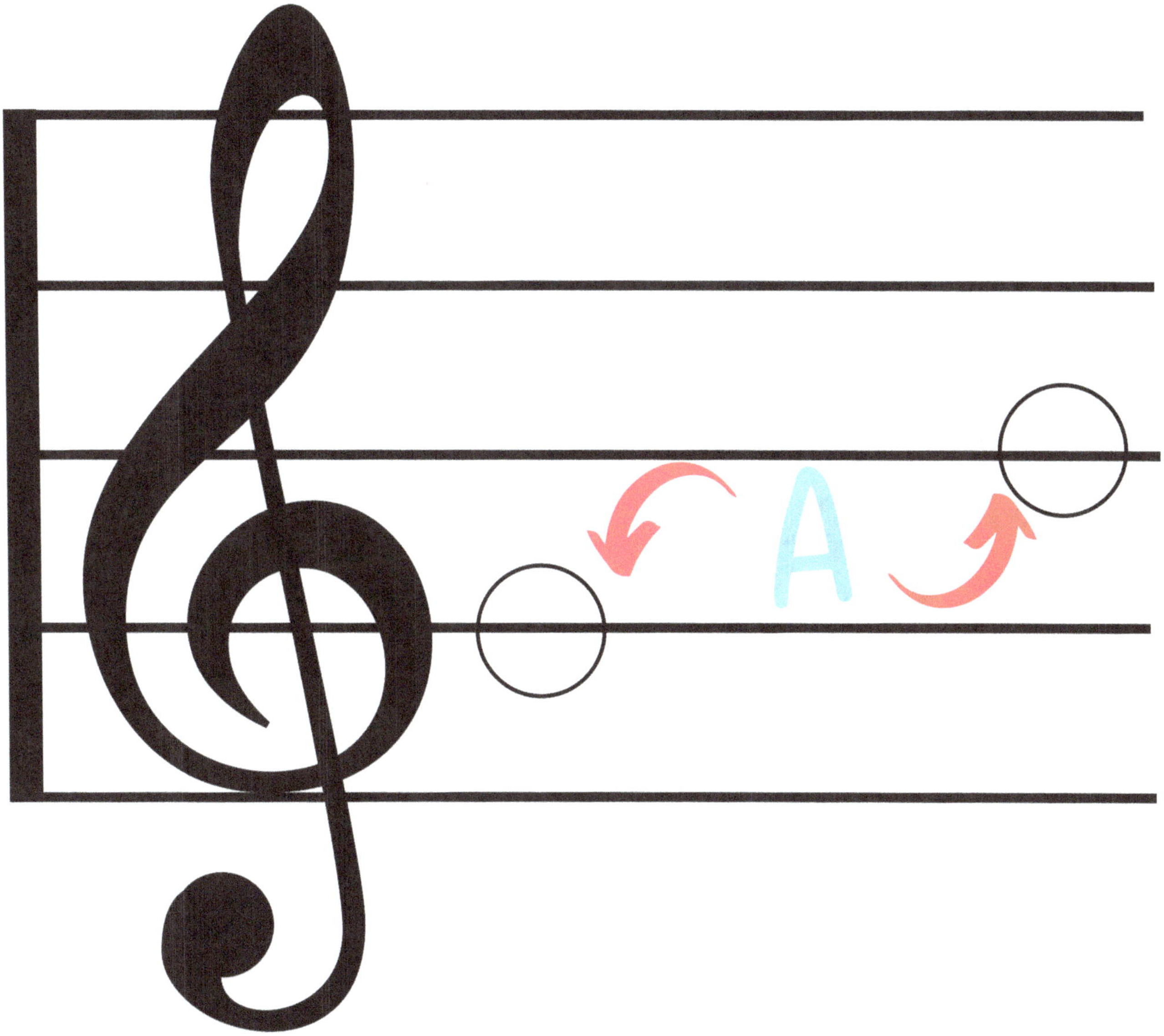

Remember, when we go **down** on the staff, we count **backwards** to find the note name. Here are the musical alphabet letters:

A B C D e f G

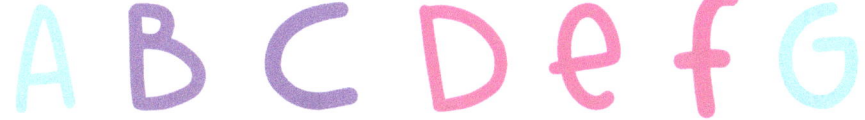

When we go **up** on the staff, we count **forwards** to find the note name.

Try again! Can you write the letter name inside the whole note?

Remember, when we go **down** on the staff, we count **backwards t**o find the note name. Here are the musical alphabet letters:

A B C D e f G

When we go **up** on the staff, we count **forwards** to find the note name.

Try again! Can you write the letter name inside the whole note?

Remember, when we go **down** on the staff, we count **backwards** to find the note name. Here are the musical alphabet letters:

A B C D e f G

When we go **up** on the staff, we count **forwards** to find the note name.

We can spell words
with the music alphabet letters!
Here's one:

Can you write the note names under the notes? What word do they spell?

Can you figure out this one? Write the note names. What word do they spell?

Your turn! Write a word using the musical alphabet. Can you draw whole notes on the correct lines and spaces?

A B C D e f G

Chapter Five:

EXPLORE THE BASS CLEF!

This is a staff with a bass clef.

A bass clef is also called a "F" clef. On this page, the "F" line is marked in green. The "F" line is in between the two dots of the bass clef.

Trace your finger on the F line.

The letter names of the bass clef spaces are ACEG.

Each letter is the first letter of a word in a silly sentence -
All Cows Eat Grass.

Can you write the letter names of the bass clef spaces?

Now can you draw a whole note (circle) on an "A" and an "E"?

Now can you draw a whole note (circle) on a "C" and a "G"?

We can find the names of the lines by counting forwards and backwards in the musical alphabet.

When we go **down** on the staff,
we count **backwards** to find the note name.

When we go **up** on the staff,
we count **forwards** to find the note name.

Your turn! Can you write the letter name inside the whole note?

When we go **down** on the staff,
we count **backwards** to find the note name.

A B C D e f G

When we go **up** on the staff,
we count **forwards** to find the note name.

Here's another one! Can you write the letter name inside the whole note?

When we go **down** on the staff,
we count **backwards** to find the note name.

A B C D e f G

When we go **up** on the staff,
we count **forwards** to find the note name.

Here's another one! Can you write the letter name inside the whole note?

When we go **down** on the staff,
we count **backwards** to find the note name.

A B C D e f G

When we go **up** on the staff,
we count **forwards** to find the note name.

We can spell words
with the music alphabet letters!
Here's one:

Can you write the note names under the notes? What word do they spell?

Can you figure out this one? Write the note names. What word do they spell?

Your turn! Write a word using the musical alphabet. Can you draw whole notes on the correct lines and spaces?

A B C D e f G

Chapter Six:

EXPLORE THE GRAND STAFF!

A Grand Staff
puts the treble and bass staffs together!

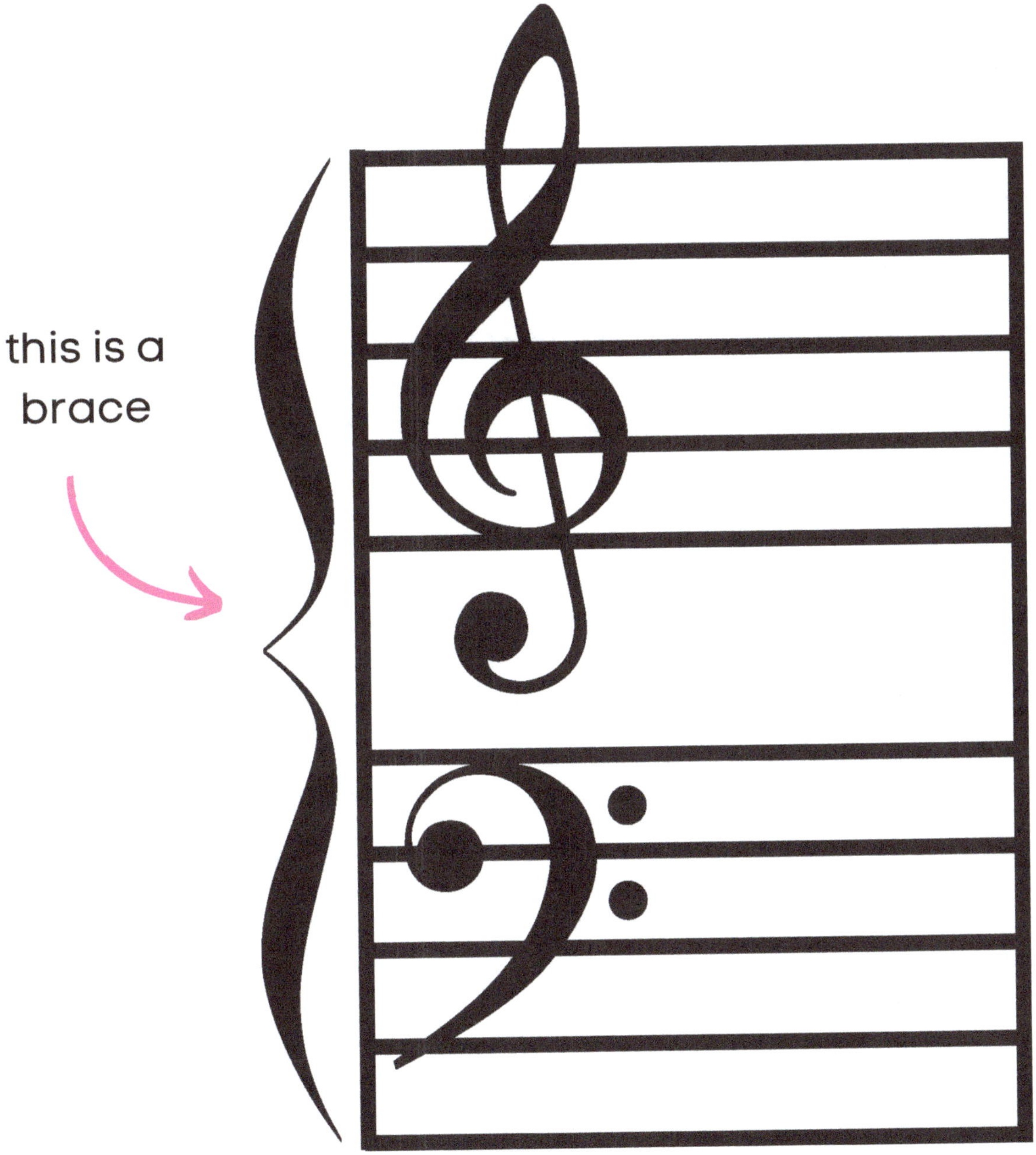

this is a
brace

Let's put all of the names of the spaces on the Grand Staff!

Can you write the names of the spaces on the Grand Staff?

Game time!

You will need:

dice

18 small pencil top erasers, or

small objects like buttons, or coins

And the staff on the next page!

(be sure your objects can fit between the lines of the staff)

RULES:

Roll the dice. Use the "secret code":

1= A or G (your pick), 2=B, 3=C, 4=D, 5=E, 6=F

Using the code, place an object on each line and space of the grand staff. Count how many times you have to roll to complete the staff. The person with the fewest rolls = winner.

Variation 1: time yourself!

Variation 2: beat someone else's time!

Variation 3: roll with your right hand for treble clef, your left hand for bass clef!

Game board

Can you color the circles using the chart below?

C = GREEN
D = YELLOW
E = RED
F = PINK
G = ORANGE
A = BLUE
B = PURPLE

There are a few notes in between the clefs.

Can you color these notes?
Use the chart below.
You will only need 3 colors!

C = GREEN
D = YELLOW
B = PURPLE

Chapter Seven:

EXPLORE INTERVALS!

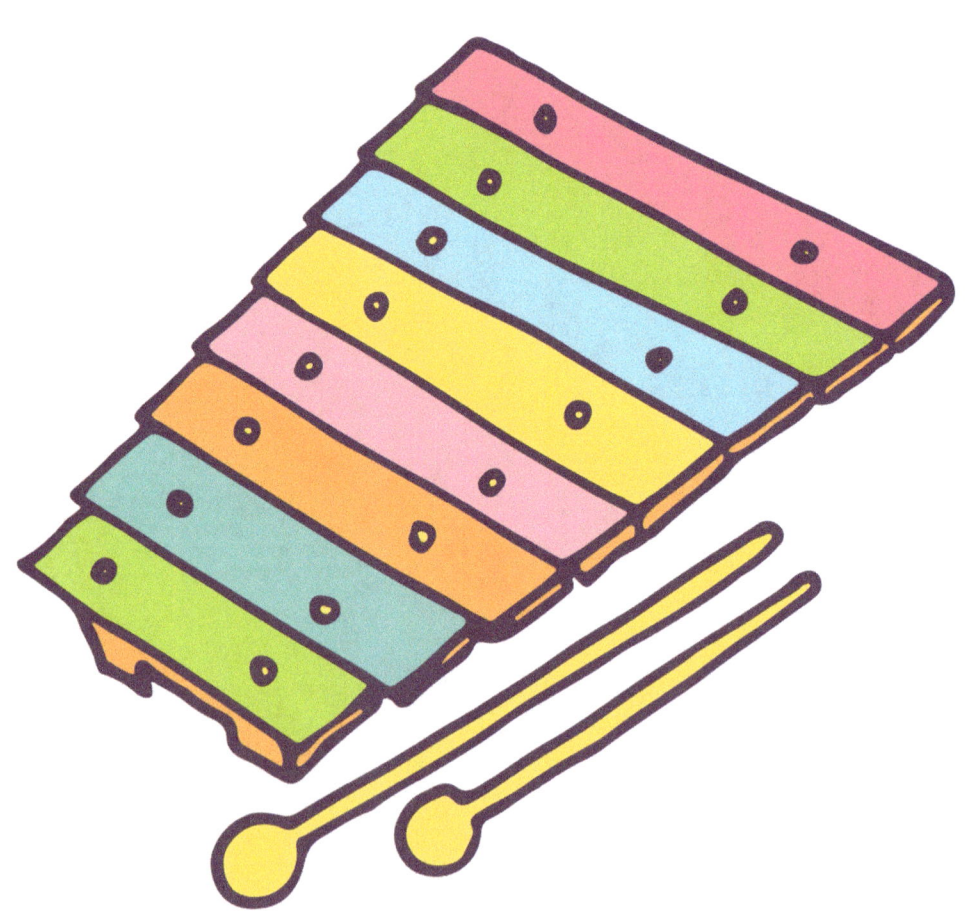

An Interval is the
distance between two notes.

We measure intervals!
Always count the first key and the last key.

1 2

This is a "2nd" or a "step".

Can you draw two dots to make a 2nd or a step on the piano keys?

This is a "3rd" or a "skip".

Can you draw dots to make a "3rd" or "skip"? Pick a different white key to begin.

This is a "4th".

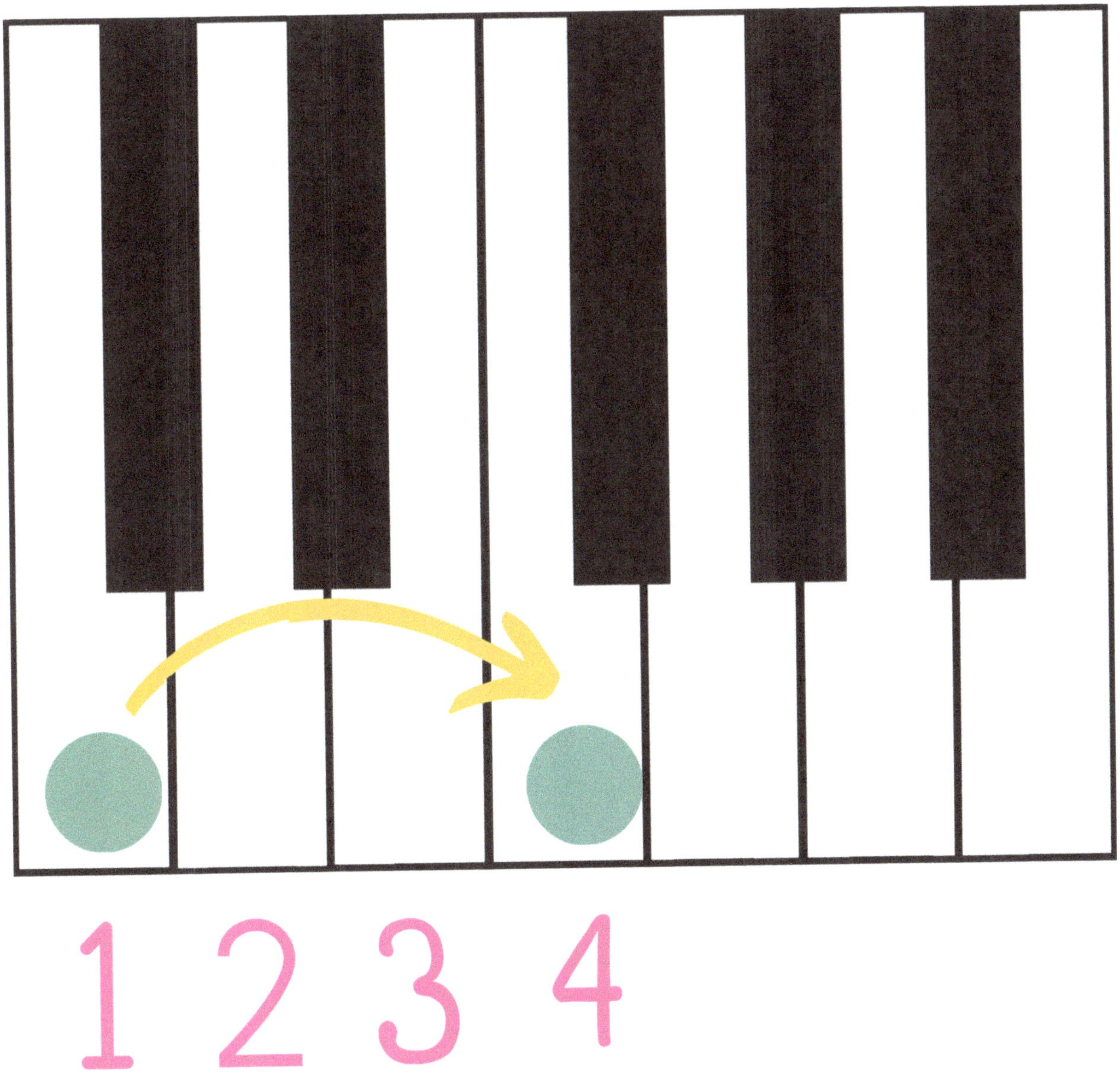

1 2 3 4

Can you draw dots to make a "4th"?
Pick a different white key to begin.

This is a "5th".

1 2 3 4 5

Can you draw dots to make a "5th"?
Pick a different white key to begin.

This is a "6th".

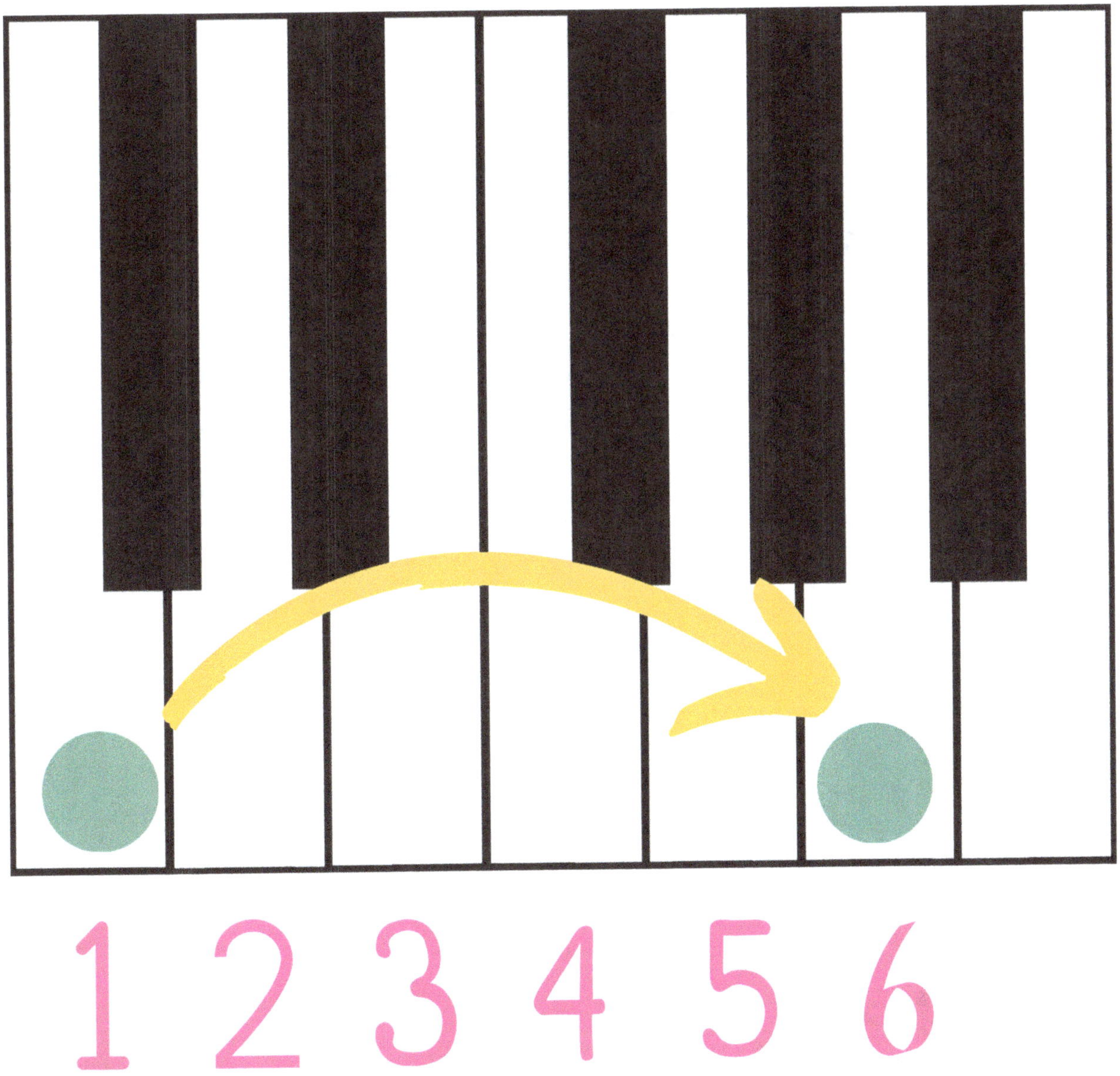

1 2 3 4 5 6

Can you draw dots to make a "6th"?
Start on C or D.

This is a "7th".

Can you draw dots to make a "7th"? Start on C.

This is a "8th".
also called an octave

1 2 3 4 5 6 7 8

And, you can keep going, counting intervals!

Can you draw dots to make an octave?

The letter names will be the same - just higher or lower!

Game time!

You will need:

 2 dice

  2 small pencil top erasers, or small objects like buttons, or coins

 An egg carton, **or** 7 small cups

 Staff paper

7 post-its, or pieces of paper, with the music alphabet written on them. ABCDEFG. Each post-it has one letter from the music alphabet.

Scan this QR code and watch the video to see how to play the game

Chapter Eight:

EXPLORE MUSICAL WORDS AND SYMBOLS!

Let's learn some musical symbols!

Dynamics tell us how loud or soft to play.

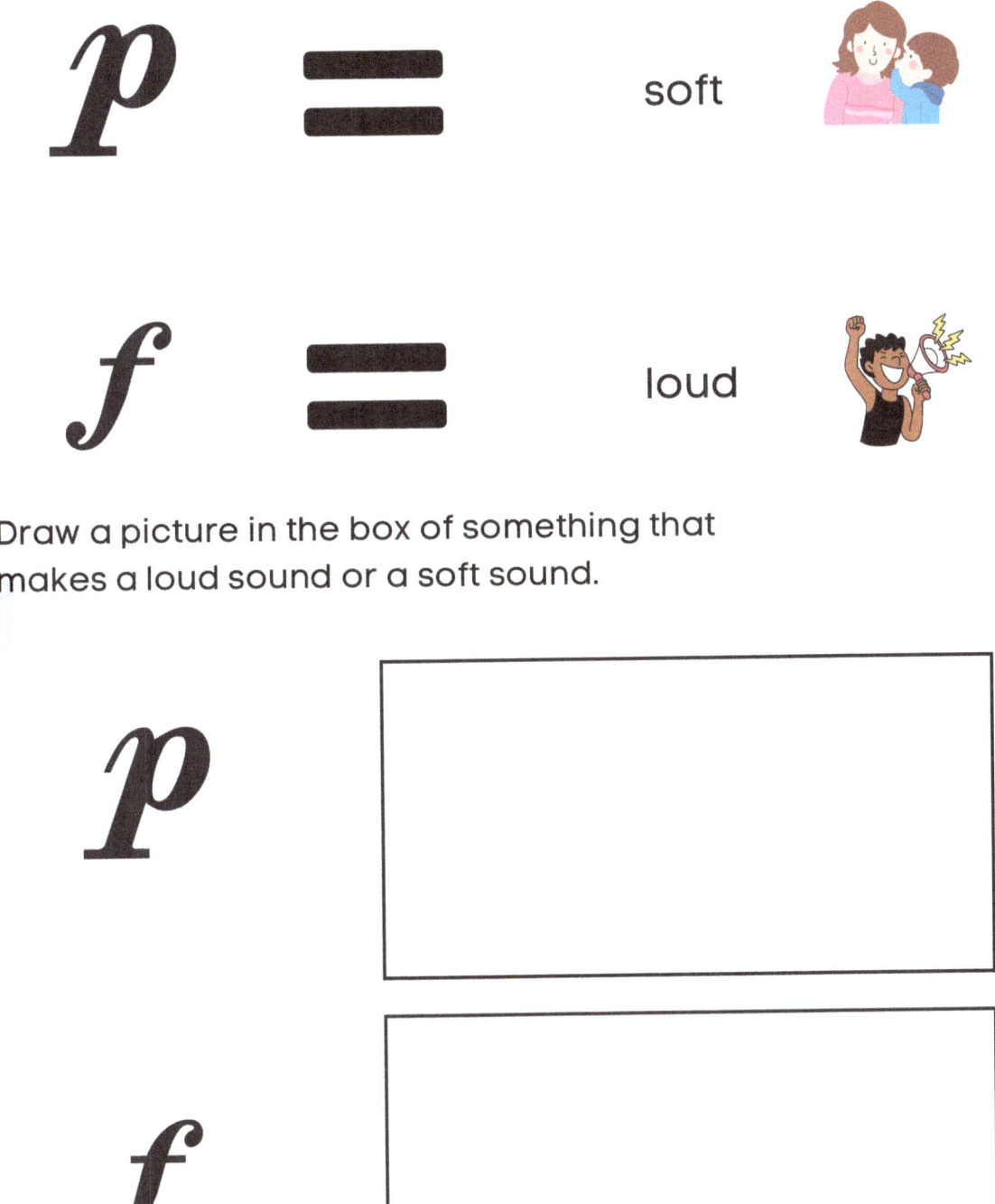

p = soft

f = loud

Draw a picture in the box of something that makes a loud sound or a soft sound.

p

f

96

More dynamics!

mp = medium soft

mf = medium loud

Let's arrange the dynamics in order,
from softest to loudest.

p   *mp*   *mf*   *f*

Write the missing dynamic marking!

p   *mp* ____ *f*

____ *mp*   *mf* ____

Remember your rhythm?

Draw lines to match the terms, notes, and number of beats!

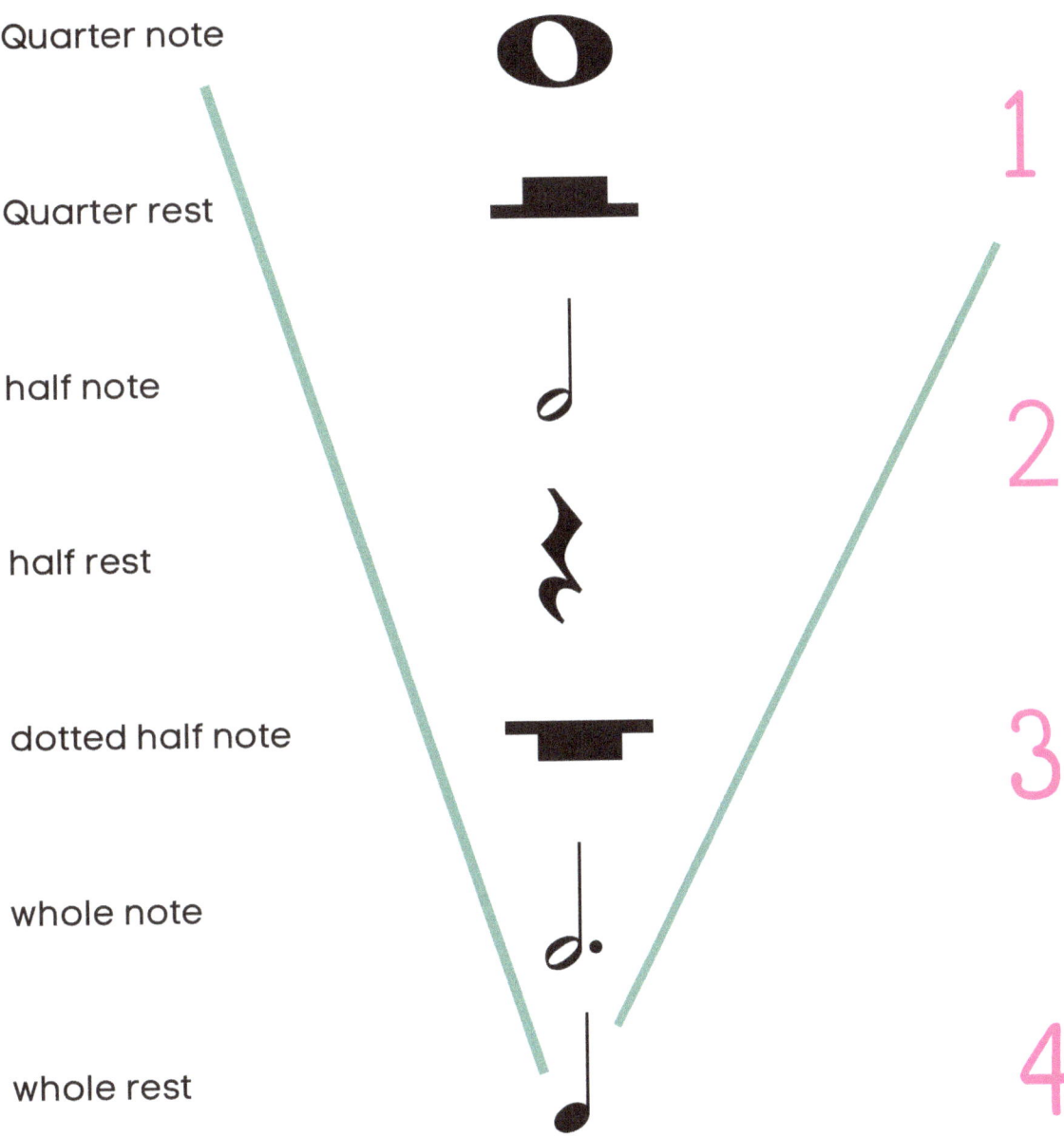

Quarter note

Quarter rest

half note

half rest

dotted half note

whole note

whole rest

1

2

3

4

Music terms you need to know!

Staff

Grand Staff

bar line

brace

measure

bass clef

treble clef

time signature

Circle the correct picture next to the music term.

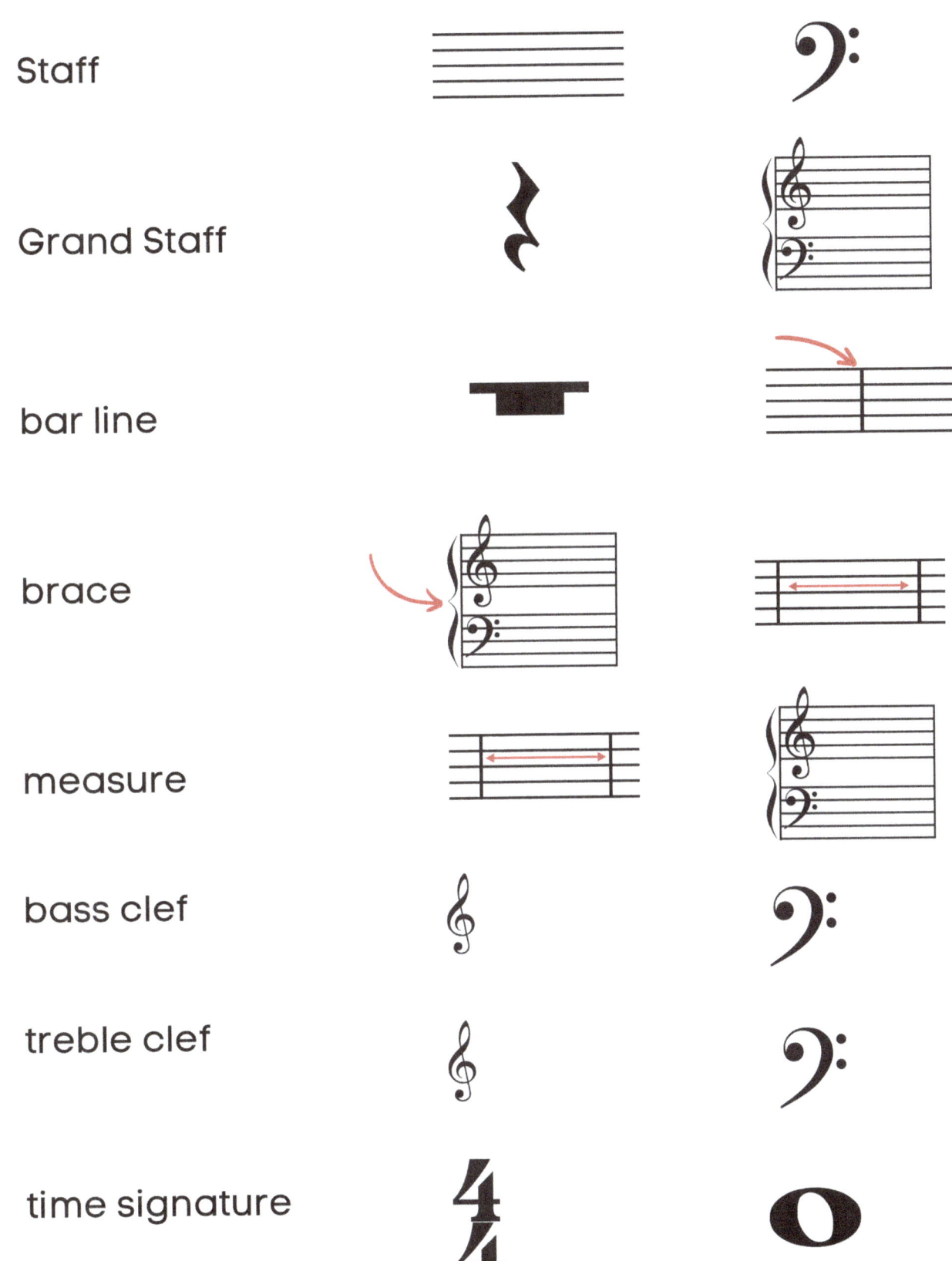

Staff

Grand Staff

bar line

brace

measure

bass clef

treble clef

time signature

Chapter Nine:

EXPLORE EASY KEY SIGNATURES!

First - we need to learn about sharps and flats!

      This is a SHARP

A sharp before a note makes it go UP to the very next key on the piano.

This is an F sharp.

When you see this,
play here:

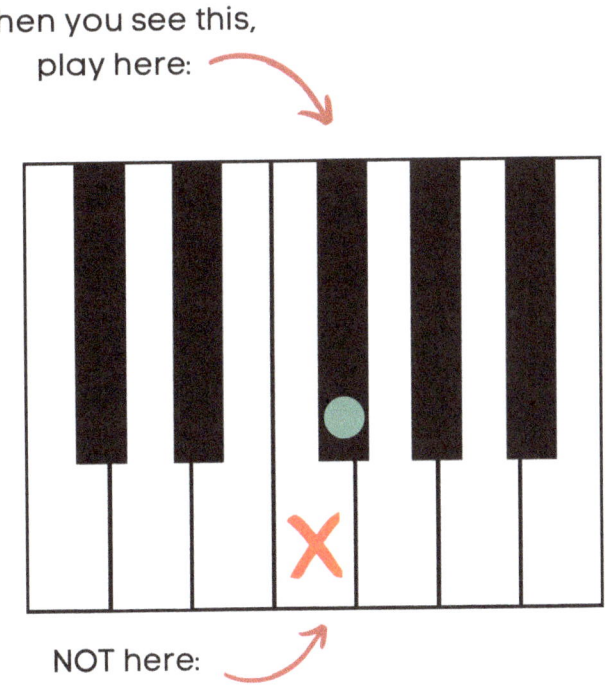

NOT here:

Now let's learn about flats!

 This is a FLAT

A flat before a note makes it go DOWN to the very next key on the piano.

This is an E flat..

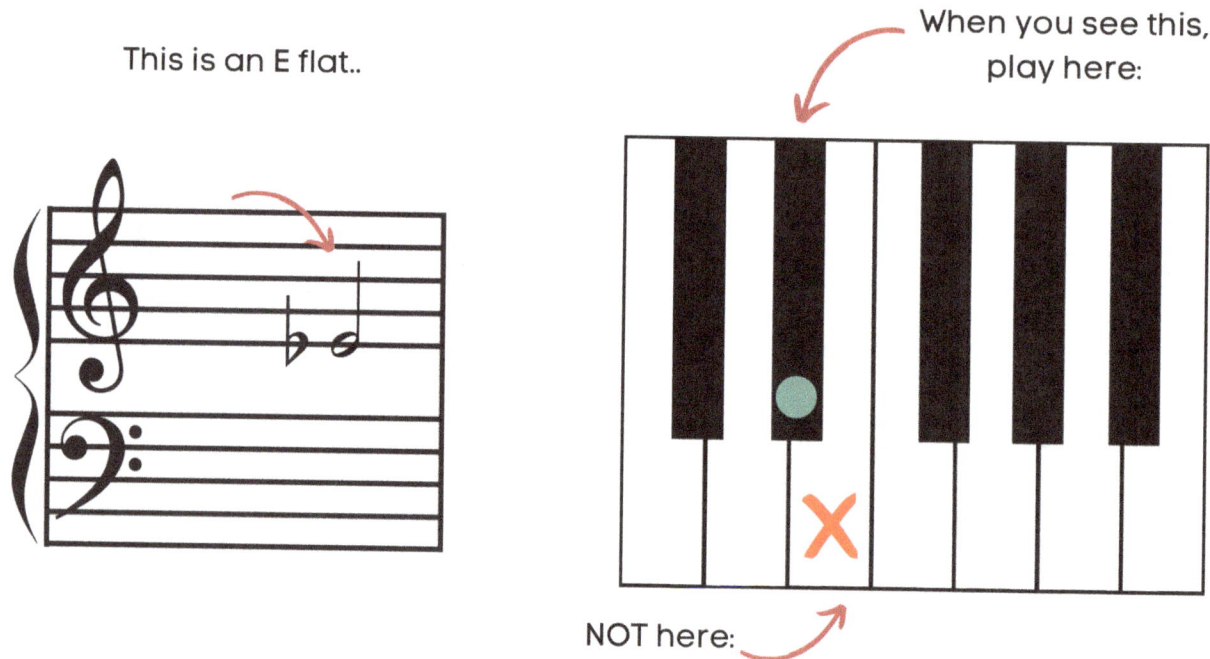

When you see this, play here:

NOT here:

Sharps and flats sometimes just SHOW up in the middle of the music. When this happens, we call that note an ACCIDENTAL.

Sometimes, there is a PLAN for all of a certain note to be sharp or flat for the ENTIRE piece!

That plan is called a KEY SIGNATURE.

The key signature always fits HERE:

If there are NO sharps or flats at the beginning, the piece is in the KEY of C Major.

If there is ONE sharp in the key signature, that piece is in the key of G Major.

Since the sharp is on the note "F", all the f's are to be played sharped.

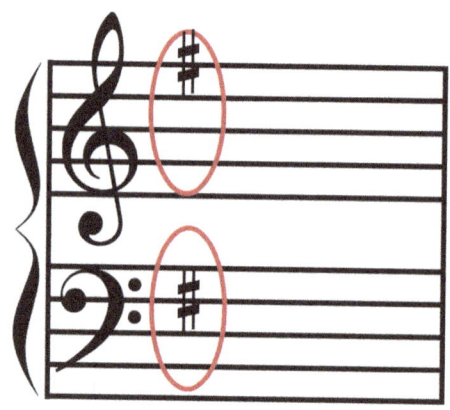

Remember - one sharp at the beginning = G Major.

If there is ONE flat in the key signature, that piece is in the key of F Major.

Since the sharp is on the note "B", all the b's are to be played flat.

Remember - one flat at the beginning = F Major.

Let's see what you have learned.

Put the name of the key in each box next to each of the pictures of a grand staff.

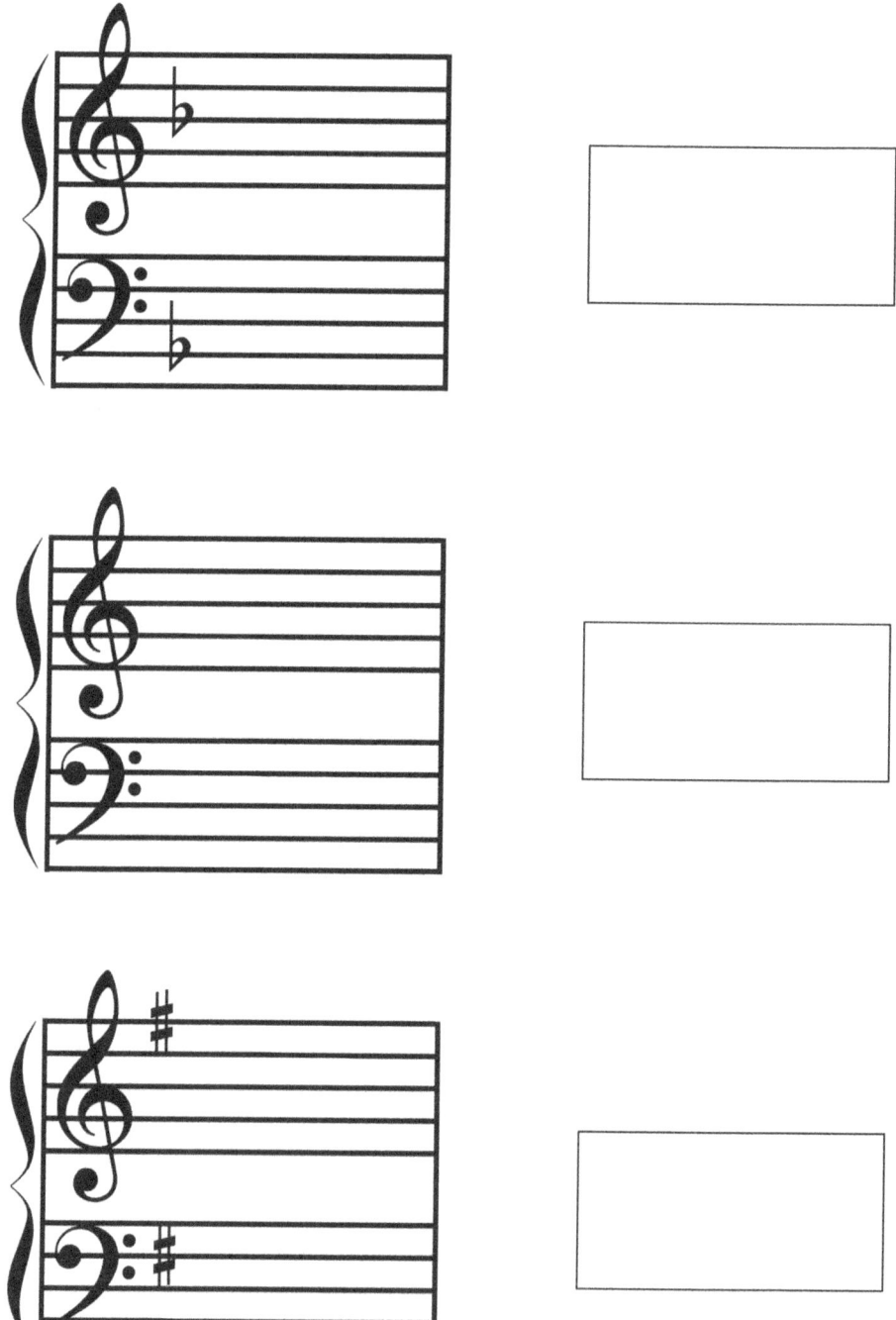

For more music fun,
check out our
Dino Notes!
Music Manuscript
Paper at Amazon